IS-212.B: Introduction to Unified Hazard Mitigation Assistance (HMA)

By

Fema

12/7/2015

Lesson 1: Introduction

Introduction

It is recommended that the lessons be completed sequentially. If they are not completed in one session, select a specific lesson from the Course Menu to resume the lesson.

There are five lessons in this course:

1. Introduction
2. Mitigation's Value to Society
3. Mitigation Planning and Projects
4. Unified HMA Grant Programs Overview
5. Unified HMA Grant Application Process

Lesson 1 Objectives

By the end of this lesson, you will be able to:

- Identify course navigation and screen features
- Describe the course goal, objectives, and course content
- Identify related courses of interest

This lesson takes approximately 7 minutes to complete.

Screen Features

- Select the **Exit** button to close this window and access the menu listing all lessons of this course. You can select any of the lessons from this menu by simply selecting the lesson title.
- Select the **Glossary** button to look up key definitions and acronyms.
- Select the **Help** button to review guidance and troubleshooting advice regarding navigating through the course.
- Track your progress by looking at the **Progress** bar at the top right of each screen. To see a numeric display, roll your mouse over the Progress bar area.
- Follow the bolded green instructions that appear on each screen in order to proceed to the next screen or complete a Knowledge Review or Activity.
- Select the **Back** or the **Next** buttons at the top and bottom of screens to move backward or forward in the lesson. **Note**: If the **Next** button is **dimmed**, you must complete an activity before you can proceed in the lesson.

Navigating Using Your Keyboard

Below are instructions for navigating through the course using your keyboard.

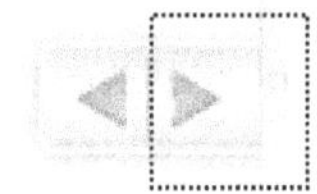

- Use the "Tab" key to move forward through each screen's navigation buttons and hyperlinks, or "Shift" + "Tab" to move backwards. A box surrounds the button that is currently selected.

- Press "Enter" to select a navigation button or hyperlink.

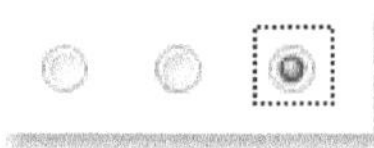

- Use the arrow keys to select answers for multiple-choice review questions or self-assessment checklists. Then tab to the "Submit" button and press "Enter" to complete a Knowledge Review or Self-Assessment.

- **Warning:** Repeatedly pressing "Tab" beyond the number of selections on the screen may cause the keyboard to lock up. Use "Ctrl" + "Tab" to deselect an element or reset to the beginning of a screen's navigation links (most often needed for screens with animations or media).

- JAWS assistive technology users can press the Ctrl key to quiet the screen reader while the course audio plays.

Receiving Credit

To receive credit for this course, you must:

Complete all of the lessons. Each lesson will take between 10 and 20 minutes to complete. It is important to allow enough time to complete the course in its entirety.

Check the length of the lesson on the overview screen.
Remember . . . YOU MUST COMPLETE THE ENTIRE COURSE TO RECEIVE CREDIT. If you have to leave the course, do not exit from the course or close your browser. If you exit from the course, you will need to start that lesson over again.

Pass the final exam. The last screen provides instructions on how to complete the final exam.

Course Goal

The purpose of this course is to educate students in the process of developing quality mitigation planning and project grant application elements for the Unified Hazard Mitigation Assistance (HMA) grant programs.

Course Content

This course consists of five lessons that can be completed according to the rules set forth
by the Emergency Management Institute.

1. Introduction
2. Mitigation's Value to Society
3. Mitigation Planning and Projects
4. Unified HMA Grant Programs Overview
5. Unified HMA Grant Application Process

Course Objectives

By the end of this course, you will be able to:

- Identify the role of mitigation and its benefits to society
- Identify and describe mitigation planning and project activities
- Identify and describe the Unified HMA grant programs
- Identify and describe the phases of the Unified HMA Federal Award life cycle

Courses of Interest

E/L/B0212 – UHMA: Developing Quality Application Elements

This course provides information for grant applicants and subapplicants on the process of
preparing quality planning and project application elements.

E/L/B0213 – UHMA: Application Review and Evaluation

This course provides participants with the knowledge and skills required to effectively
review and evaluate subapplications submitted to FEMA's mitigation programs. This
course will provide a general overview of how a Federal award is issued.

E/L/B0214 – UHMA: Project Implementation and Closeout

This course provides participants with the knowledge and skills required to effectively
implement and close out a project.

E0276 – Benefit-Cost Analysis: Entry-Level Training

This course is designed to be an introduction to the fundamental concepts of benefit-cost analysis (BCA). Participants will learn how to obtain data and conduct BCAs using the basic versions of the various hazard modules.

E0344 – Mitigation Planning for Tribal Officials

This course provides Indian Tribal members and their representatives with an overview of FEMA's mitigation programs, outlines tribal mitigation responsibilities, and discusses opportunities for achieving mitigation successes.

IS-393.a – Introduction to Hazard Mitigation

This course provides an introduction to hazard mitigation for those who are new to emergency management and are interested in reducing hazard risks in their jurisdictions.

Lesson 1 Summary

In Lesson 1 you learned to:

- Identify course navigation and screen features
- Describe the course goal, objectives, and course content
- Identify related courses of interest

Lesson 2: Mitigation's Value to Society

Lesson 2 Objectives

By the end of this lesson, you will be able to:

- Define mitigation
- Identify how mitigation benefits society
- Demonstrate the economic benefits of mitigation projects

This lesson takes approximately 12 minutes to complete.

Definition of Mitigation

The term **"mitigation"** refers to those capabilities necessary to reduce loss of life and property by lessening the impact of disasters. Mitigation capabilities include, but are not limited to:

- Community-wide risk reduction projects
- Efforts to improve the resilience of critical infrastructure and key resource lifelines
- Risk reduction for specific vulnerabilities from natural hazards or acts of terrorism
- Initiatives to reduce future risks after a disaster has occurred

What is Mitigation's Value to Society?

Mitigation creates safer communities and saves money for:

- Individuals
- Government
- Society

Building and maintaining structures that incorporate mitigation strategies saves money for individuals through:

- Improved insurance rates
- Lower post-disaster rebuilding/replacement costs

State, local and Indian Tribal governments that incorporate mitigation strategies avoid or reduce damages to public infrastructure. Society as a whole benefits from improved resiliency because fewer resources are needed for response and recovery.

Studying Mitigation's Value

Studies have documented the cost-effectiveness of mitigation activities. Communities with established hazard mitigation programs and sound building codes experience the greatest benefits. New or remodeled buildings are more likely to incorporate privately-funded mitigation design measures.

During the grant application phase, a **Benefit-Cost Analysis** is used to estimate savings of a proposed mitigation measure realized during future disaster events.

A **Loss Avoidance Study** is used to determine mitigation's actual value to society. This type of study looks at mitigation measures and their calculated savings after completed projects have been tested by disaster events.

Studying Mitigation's Value (continued)

The Multihazard Mitigation Council (MMC) and Congressional Budget Office (CBO) completed studies examining hundreds of projects to determine how cost-effective mitigation projects provided value.

Multihazard Mitigation Council Study

In 2005, the MMC completed a loss avoidance study using a random sampling of mitigation projects. The Council found that an investment of $3.5 billion saved $14 billion, which translates to $4 saved for every $1 spent.

Congressional Budget Office Study

A study published in September 2007 by the CBO analyzed projects that were funded by FEMA's Pre-Disaster Mitigation (PDM) Program to determine the extent to which the projects might reduce expected losses from future natural disasters. The CBO report built on the results of the MMC study. Results from this study showed that the total dollar value of the expected reduction in disaster losses from PDM-funded projects exceeded the projects' costs. On average, future losses were reduced by about $3 for every $1 spent.

Studying Mitigation's Value (continued)

A Loss Avoidance Study (LAS) can be completed for projects after they are finished and have been "tested" by a hazard event. The following are a few examples of LASs:

Birmingham, Alabama

Completed in 2000, an LAS in Birmingham, Alabama analyzed 735 acquisitions on Village Creek, which was subject to flooding. This study showed that the acquisitions implemented by the U.S. Army Corps of Engineers (USACE) at a cost of $36 million had avoided losses of more than $60 million by the completion of the study. This investment yielded a losses avoided ratio of 1.50. Additionally, further acquisitions by FEMA and the City of Birmingham have avoided direct losses of $3.4 million for an investment of $7 million in less than 2 years. These numbers were adjusted to 2004 dollars.

Georgia

In 2010, FEMA partnered with the Georgia Emergency Management Agency (GEMA) to conduct an LAS to evaluate the cost-effectiveness of several mitigation projects. For the study, FEMA and GEMA selected 29 building modification projects consisting of 172 total structures in Chattooga, Cobb, DeKalb, Douglas, and Gwinnett counties that were completed between 1997 and 2009. All but one project involved residential buildings that had been acquired and demolished. The other project involved the demolition of a school and then rebuilding it outside the 500-year floodplain. The aggregate losses avoided for the 172 buildings were valued at $27,426,369, and the aggregate project investment was valued at $48,885,368 (both values in 2010 dollars), resulting in a losses avoided ratio of 0.56 for all storm events studied.

Northern California

An LAS conducted in Northern California examined the effectiveness of HMA-eligible minor flood control mitigation projects. Six projects were included in the study, which was completed in July 2008. An initial investment of $48.1 million was made for these mitigation projects. The losses avoided from actual events were $46.9 million, based on 2007 dollars. This yielded a 0.97 losses avoided ratio.

Sonoma County, CA

This study examined 205 structures that were elevated to avoid flooding in Sonoma County, California. Completed in April 2008 and based on dollars adjusted to 2007, the findings showed that an investment of $14.2 million resulted in losses avoided of $13.5 million. The losses avoided ratio was 0.96.

Oregon

Low-lying areas between the Coast Range and the Pacific Ocean in southwestern Oregon are particularly vulnerable to severe flooding. The City of Tillamook, which is located in this region, has repeatedly experienced severe floods. In response, the City and County of Tillamook implemented a number of flood mitigation projects to reduce the damage from future floods. The projects consisted of the acquisition, elevation, and relocation of floodprone buildings. The aggregate losses avoided were valued at $3.1 million, and the aggregate project cost was valued at approximately $4.7 million (both values in 2009 dollars), resulting in a losses avoided ratio of 0.66. FEMA estimates that elevation projects are estimated to have an average useful life of 30 years and that acquisition projects have a useful life of 100 years. The majority of the projects were implemented after 2003, which is only 6 years into their useful life.

Washington

The 1996 floods in the State of Washington caused severe damage and were declared a Major Disaster by the President. Following this disaster, local governments, with State and Federal assistance, completed a number of flood mitigation projects to reduce future damage from similar floods. These projects included the Tributary 0170 Drainage Improvement Project in the City of Issaquah and the installation of the Old Stilly Flood Drainage Gate near the City of Stanwood. The flood on January 7, 2009, was similar in size to the 1996 flood, affected both cities, and caused significantly less damage in the vicinity of these two projects than the 1996 floods. Consequently, FEMA partnered with the State of Washington to conduct a loss avoidance study of the two projects. The value of the losses avoided for the two projects combined was $1,204,058, and the total cost of the two projects was $1,245,726 (both values in 2009 dollars), resulting in a losses avoided ratio of 0.97. Localized flood reduction projects are estimated to have an average useful life of 30 to 50 years. Both projects were implemented only 2 years before the 2009 flooding.

Wisconsin

In response to frequent flooding, the local governments in Kenosha, Jefferson, and Crawford counties, with Federal and State assistance, acquired a total of 92 repetitive-loss properties from 1989 to 2008. FEMA calculated the value of the losses that had been avoided by the implementation of the mitigation projects and compared the losses avoided with the acquisition costs. The aggregate losses avoided were valued at $14.5 million, and the aggregate project cost was valued at approximately $11 million (both values in 2009 dollars), resulting in a losses avoided ratio of 1.32.

Studying Mitigation's Value (continued)

In general, mitigation activities have been found to save money.
They promote sound development through rigorous building standards and local governing ordinances such as:

- Flood Damage Prevention Ordinances
- Local, State, or International Building Codes
- Wildland/Urban Interface Codes

These ordinances all reduce vulnerability to disasters.

Mitigation speeds recovery. After a disaster, mitigation can reduce post-disaster disruption and allow quicker rebuilding.

To summarize, mitigation:

- Creates safer communities
- Saves money for individuals and communities
- Promotes sound development
- Speeds recovery

Link to Building Codes: http://www.iccsafe.org/Pages/default.aspx

Lesson 2 Summary

In Lesson 2 you learned to:

- Define mitigation
- Identify how mitigation benefits society
- Demonstrate the economic benefits of mitigation projects

Lesson 3: Mitigation Planning and Projects

Lesson Objectives

By the end of this lesson, you will be able to:

- Identify the importance of mitigation planning
- Identify the steps required for completing a mitigation plan
- Highlight resources available for mitigation planning
- Recognize the connections between mitigation plans and projects

This lesson takes approximately **20 minutes** to complete.

Mitigation Plans

Mitigation Planning:

- Is the first phase in the mitigation process.
- Helps establish the mitigation strategy and outline priorities for identifying mitigation activities.
- Is required to receive project funding.
- Identifies potential projects relative to hazard risk.

Mitigation Plans (continued)

Approved mitigation plans are a requirement for all of Unified HMA programs. These requirements may be found in the following CFR citations:

- CFR 206.434(b), 201.4(a), and 201.6(a)(1): Hazard Mitigation Grant Program (HMGP)
- CFR 201.4(a) and 201.6(a)(2): Pre-Disaster Mitigation (PDM)
- CFR 79.6(b): Flood Mitigation Assistance (FMA)

Select this link to view 44 CFR

Mitigation Plans (continued)

Mitigation planning contributes to resilient communities by:

- Building partnerships
- Establishing project priorities relative to hazard risk
- Making cost-effective decisions on actions to reduce risk
- Reducing future losses and facilitating recovery
- Supporting successful project applications
- Facilitating project funding

Mitigation Plans (continued)

Mitigation planning also benefits the community by:

- Educating local officials about hazard risk and implications for development decisions.
- Making businesses aware of hazard risks and options for making them safer.
- Enabling developers to identify hazard areas to avoid and encouraging builders to use designs and materials that will reduce the potential for damage.

Mitigation Plans (continued)

For planning guidance, please go to http://www.fema.gov.

State Standard Mitigation Plan

A State Standard Mitigation Plan must include coordination with adopted local mitigation plans and assurances that the State will comply with all appropriate Federal statutes and regulations. This plan establishes the process for the State government to:

- Define their hazards
- Explain how they will deal with those hazards
- Set criteria for prioritizing communities in that State to receive FEMA planning and project Federal awards

The plan must be adopted and implemented by the State. State governments must have an approved Standard Mitigation Plan in order for communities in that State to receive any Unified HMA Federal awards. The State Standard Mitigation Plan is valid for five years from FEMA approval.

State Enhanced Mitigation Plan

A State Enhanced Mitigation Plan requires increased responsibility for mitigation planning and program oversight. An enhanced plan includes all elements of a standard plan, PLUS it addresses the:

- Integration with other State or regional planning initiatives
- Ability to implement the plan
- Demonstrated effective use of existing mitigation programs
- Commitment to a comprehensive State mitigation program

An approved State Enhanced Mitigation Plan makes the State government eligible for a higher level of post-disaster Hazard Mitigation Grant Program (HMGP) funding—up to

20% versus 15% for States with Standard Mitigation Plans. This plan is valid for five years from FEMA approval.

Indian Tribal Mitigation Plan

Effective on October 1, 2008, 44 CFR 201.7 was implemented to better meet the needs of Indian Tribal governments. These regulations allow Indian Tribal governments to demonstrate the ability to apply for and manage Federal award funds as direct applicants to FEMA through the Indian Tribal Enhanced Mitigation Plan.

Prior to this date, Indian Tribal governments were given the option to meet the requirements of a State or of a local mitigation plan. Those plans are still valid until they expire.

The Indian Tribal Mitigation Plan establishes the process for the Indian Tribal government to define and address its hazard risks. Documentation of the planning process is required and should include:

- Risk assessment
- Mitigation strategy
- Plan maintenance

This plan must be adopted and implemented by the Indian Tribal government in order for the Tribe to be eligible for most Unified HMA Federal awards. If the Tribe desires a subrecipient status so that they will have less responsibility for oversight, then the plan is submitted to the State. For Recipient status, the plan can be directly submitted to FEMA and, if approved, comes with increased responsibility and oversight. Once approved, Indian Tribal Mitigation Plans are valid for five years.

Indian Tribal Enhanced Mitigation Plan

To qualify for Enhanced Mitigation Plan status, the Indian Tribal Enhanced Mitigation Plan must meet all of the requirements under 44 CFR 201.7 plus the requirements of the State Enhanced Mitigation Plan.

Local Mitigation Plan

Similar to an Indian Tribal Mitigation Plan, a Local Mitigation Plan documents the planning process, which includes a:

- Risk assessment
- Mitigation strategy to prioritize projects based on risk
- Plan maintenance strategy

Local multi-jurisdictional plans must be adopted by all participating jurisdictions. Tribes may choose to participate in a local multi-jurisdictional mitigation plan. However, all participating jurisdictions must fulfill all planning requirements to be eligible for certain grant programs. Local mitigation plans are valid for five years.

Mitigation Plans (continued)

Planning Process Description
A description of the planning process must be included to show who participated on a planning team, how the public was invited to provide input, and other important criteria.

Risk Assessment
The risk assessment process provides the foundation for the rest of the mitigation planning process. The four basic components of the risk assessment are to: 1) Identify hazards; 2) Profile hazard events; 3) Inventory assets at risk; and 4) Estimate losses.

Mitigation Strategy
A mitigation strategy provides the blueprint for reducing the losses identified in the risk assessment. The strategy must include goals that are based on the risk assessment, and they should be consistent with goals from other State or local jurisdictions' plans and policies.

Plan Maintenance Process
Risk changes over time, and mitigation plans should change along with it. The plan maintenance process establishes a method and schedule for monitoring, evaluating, and updating the plan. This includes a review of goals, objectives, and actions that have been completed.

Plan Adoption Process
The plan adoption process is how the jurisdiction formally adopts the mitigation plan. Local mitigation plans must be adopted in order for jurisdictions included in the plan to be eligible for mitigation project funding.

Mitigation Plans: Resources

Most communities have access to resources that can provide technical assistance in the mitigation planning process, including:

- Staff with planning, engineering, and scientific expertise
- Geographic Information Systems (GIS)
- State/Indian Tribal staff
- State Hazard Mitigation Officer (SHMO)
- Indian Tribal Hazard Mitigation Officer (THMO)
- Geologist and climatologist
- Hurricane or earthquake program managers
- Floodplain manager
- Local universities and colleges
- Regional planning associations
- Private-sector consultants
- Emergency management personnel
- Public works/utilities personnel
- Federal partners, such as U.S. Forest Service (USFS), National Oceanic and Atmospheric Administration (NOAA), or U.S. Geological Survey (USGS)
- Public or local residents

Mitigation Plans: Resources (continued)

Valuable mitigation planning resources are FEMA's Mitigation Planning How-To Guides. There are nine "How-To" guides that address the activities and issues involved in each required component of a mitigation plan.

For more information on these guides, please go to:
http://www.fema.gov/hazard-mitigation-planning-resources#1

Common Hazards in the U.S.

How does mitigation planning link to the grant application process?

The first planning step is to identify the hazards that may affect the community. Some of the common hazards that occur in the United States are listed below.

Tornadoes: Each year, hundreds of tornadoes strike the central part of the United States and Gulf coast, although they can occur in virtually any part of the country. You can use tornado count and severe weather statistics to judge the importance of tornadoes in your mitigation planning effort.

Floods: Floods and flash floods happen in every state. Many homes and businesses are at risk from flood damage. If your community has suffered flood damage, there are probably flood studies and maps that identify areas of different levels of flood risk.

Hurricanes: Hurricanes affect the United States in most years. If you live on or near the Atlantic or Gulf coasts, your community may have a history of hurricane damage. As the last decade has shown, aside from coastal flooding, hurricanes can also cause extensive inland flooding and wind damage.

Wildfires: If your community has houses and businesses located near forested areas or rural areas with substantial vegetation, wildfire may be a threat.

Earthquakes: Earthquakes are another hazard that we face in the United States. Although the West Coast is most identified with earthquake hazards, many other regions also face significant risks from seismic activity.

Risk Assessment Tool

After identifying the hazards, the next step is to evaluate the relative risk of each hazard's impact on the community. This is called risk assessment. Risk assessment looks at how frequent a specific hazard occurs and how large (in intensity or magnitude) it is and then examines the exposure and vulnerability of assets at risk.

One resource for risk assessment is the Hazards-US Risk and Vulnerability Determination Tool (HAZUS-MH), available on the **FEMA HAZUS** website.

HAZUS-MH is a powerful risk assessment program used for analyzing potential losses from floods, hurricane winds, and earthquakes. HAZUS-MH combines current scientific and engineering knowledge with the latest geographic information systems (GIS) technology to produce estimates of hazard-related damage.

Mitigation Plans

Mitigation plans must include a *mitigation strategy* that identifies actions to reduce specific risks that were identified in the *risk assessment*.

Mitigation project types must be outlined in the mitigation plan. On the next three slides, you will have to correctly match a picture of a mitigation activity to the mitigation project type.

Lesson 3 Summary

In Lesson 3 you learned to:

- Identify the importance of mitigation planning
- Identify the steps required for completing a mitigation plan
- Highlight resources available for mitigation planning
- Recognize the connections between mitigation plans and projects

Lesson 4: Unified HMA Grant Programs Overview

Lesson Objectives

By the end of this lesson, you will be able to:

- Identify the Unified HMA grant programs
- Identify common requirements and basic elements of applications
- Recognize the benefits of unifying the HMA grant programs
- Identify the two electronic application submittal systems

This lesson takes approximately 10 minutes to complete.

Unified HMA Grant Programs

You have seen examples of mitigation projects that saved lives and property for individuals, communities, and society. These projects can be expensive and require financial support to accomplish.

This is where funding from FEMA's Unified Hazard Mitigation Assistance (HMA) grant programs is helpful. The three HMA programs fund a range of mitigation activities.

The ***Hazard Mitigation Grant Program (HMGP)*** provides Federal awards for long-term hazard mitigation projects following a major disaster declaration. The purpose of the program is to reduce the loss of life and property in future disasters by funding mitigation measures during or after the recovery phase of a natural disaster.

The ***Pre-Disaster Mitigation (PDM) Program*** provides Federal awards for hazard mitigation planning and the implementation of mitigation projects prior to a disaster event. These plans and projects reduce overall risks to the population and structures, while also reducing reliance on funding from actual disaster declarations.

The ***Flood Mitigation Assistance (FMA) Program*** grant program provides funding for cost-effective measures that reduce or eliminate the long-term risk of flood damage to buildings, manufactured homes, and other structures insured under the National Flood Insurance Program (NFIP). The goal of the FMA program is to reduce or eliminate claims under the NFIP through mitigation activities.

Common Program Elements

Eligible applicants apply for one or more of the Unified HMA grant programs to help them fund mitigation projects. Unified HMA grant programs include these three common elements:

1. NFIP Participation
2. Project Requirements
3. Basic Application Elements

Common Program Elements (continued)

NFIP Participation

The NFIP requires communities to manage development in their floodplains. A project in an identified Special Flood Hazard Area (SFHA) must be located within a community that is:

- Participating in the NFIP
- In good standing with NFIP
  (not suspended or withdrawn)
- Any structure mitigated must have an NFIP policy

The only exception to this policy is the Pre-Disaster Mitigation (PDM) program pertaining to Federally-recognized Indian Tribal governments. If an Indian Tribal government has been issued a floodplain map and is not participating in the NFIP, then it may be eligible to receive a PDM planning award. The purpose of the planning grant is to provide Indian Tribal governments with the information, resources, and incentives that will enable them to take the necessary steps to participate in the NFIP. Once it is a part of the NFIP, the Indian Tribal government will be eligible for PDM project awards.

Common Program Elements (continued)

Project Requirements

All projects require:

- FEMA-approved State or Indian Tribal plan
- Technical Feasibility
- Cost-effectiveness
- Environmental and Historic Preservation (EHP)

Common Program Elements (continued)

Basic Application Elements:

All Unified HMA grant applications must include:

- Scope of Work
- Work Schedule/Timeline
- Cost Estimate/Budget

These elements will be addressed in more depth in course E/L/B212 - Unified Hazard Mitigation Assistance: Developing Quality Application Elements.

Electronic Application Systems

HMA applications are currently processed in two different systems:

- Under **HMGP**, paper-based applications are entered into and processed in the NEMIS HMGP System. For more information about this system, access the FAQ or the User Manual.
- Under the **PDM** and **FMA** programs, applications are processed through the Electronic Grants (*e*Grants) Management System. *e*Grants streamlines the application process by providing State and local governments the ability to apply for and manage their applications over the Internet. For more information about this system, access the *e*Grants page on the FEMA website.

FEMA-Approved Mitigation Plans

All applicants must have a FEMA-approved State mitigation plan (Standard or Enhanced) or an Indian Tribal mitigation plan by the application deadline date to be eligible to apply for and receive project funding under the HMA programs.

Subapplicants must have an approved local or Indian Tribal mitigation plan.

For the HMGP, FEMA may grant an exception to the local hazard mitigation plan requirement in extraordinary circumstances, when justification is provided. If this exception is granted, a local mitigation plan must be approved by FEMA within 12 months of issuing the project subaward.

Lesson 4 Summary

In Lesson 4 you learned to:

- Identify the Unified HMA grant programs
- Identify common requirements and basic elements of applications
- Recognize the benefits of unifying the HMA grant programs
- Identify the two application submittal programs

Lesson 5: Unified HMA Grant Application Process

Lesson Objectives

By the end of this lesson, you will be able to:

- Identify the life cycle of Unified HMA Federal awards
- Learn of additional training that is offered on the Federal award life cycle process

Federal Award Life Cycle: Activity Identification

The Federal award process begins with identification of a mitigation activity. This is where the planning process links to the grant application process.

Activity identification includes:

- Designating the activity as related to mitigation planning or a mitigation project.
- Identifying the Federal award type: planning award or project award.
- If the activity is a project, scoping the project and developing pre-application information.

Activity Identification is addressed in detail in course E/L/B0212 Unified Hazard Mitigation Assistance: Developing Quality Application Elements.

Federal Award Life Cycle: Application Development

The next step following identification of the mitigation activity is the development and submission of the grant application. This includes:

- Developing the Scope of Work
- Developing the Work Plan
- Creating the Cost Estimate and Project Budget

There are some differences in the application requirements for planning awards and for project awards. For more information on application requirements see the current Unified HMA Guidance at http://www.fema.gov.

Application Development is addressed in detail in course E/L/B0212 Unified Hazard Mitigation Assistance: Developing Quality Application Elements.

Federal Award Life Cycle: Application Review and Evaluation & Federal Award

After the application is completed and submitted, the next steps are to review the application. If it is approvable and if funding is available, it is awarded.

Application Review and Evaluation & Federal Award are addressed in detail in course E/L/B0213 Unified Hazard Mitigation Assistance: Application Review and Evaluation.

Federal Award Life Cycle: Activity Implementation and Federal Award Closeout

After your project is awarded, it doesn't mean your work is finished. Managing the Federal award and implementing the project can be the most difficult part of the entire Federal award life cycle. Projects must be implemented in accordance with the Federal award requirements.

Training is available on both the activity implementation and closeout process:

- E/L/B0214 Unified Hazard Mitigation Assistance: Project Implementation and Closeout
- State and Indian Tribal governments may also offer grants management courses

Lesson 5 Summary

In Lesson 5 you learned to:

- Identify the life cycle of Unified HMA Federal awards
- Learn of additional training that is offered on the Federal award life cycle process

Course Summary

In this course, you learned to:

- Identify the role of mitigation and its benefits to society
- Identify and describe mitigation planning and project activities
- Identify and describe the Unified HMA grant programs
- Identify and describe the phases of the Unified HMA Federal Award life cycle

www.ingramcontent.com/pod-product-compliance
Lightning Source LLC
Chambersburg PA
CBHW081325250726
48662CB00008B/2760